THE BOYS OF BLUEHILL

Eiléan
Ní
Chuilleanáin

WAKE FOREST UNIVERSITY PRESS

The Boys of Bluehill

WINSTON-SALEM, NORTH CAROLINA

First North American edition

For permission, write to
Wake Forest University Press
Post Office Box 7333
Winston-Salem, NC 27109
wfupress.wfu.edu
wfupress@wfu.edu

ISBN 978-1-930630-72-7 (paperback)

Library of Congress Catalog Number 2014959875

Designed and typeset by Quemadura

Publication of this book was generously
supported by the Boyle Family Fund.

THE BOYS OF BLUEHILL

AN INFORMATION

I returned to that narrow street
where I used to stand and listen
to the chat from kitchen or parlour, filtered
through rotten tiles. I thought
the rough walls seemed higher than before.
My cheek against the stone, I noted the new door
since last I'd been there, began to count the years,

to count the questions I couldn't ask now
(Did you sit apart? Had you washed your hands
before entering the room? Was the water laced
with vinegar? What did you say while it thundered?
And what did you say when you went out
so the crowds that danced at the wedding
would not know your whole story?)

They are dancing still beside the river,
and now I see her climbing towards me
up the long flight of steps that winds
beside the fever hospital,
in her covered basket, the makings
of the meal. I had never
found out the certain day.

And now I must not ask, where did you buy the bread,
and did they guess, in the shop where you got the duck-eggs,
that you had a guest? Along the alleys
the wind whispered to me: open your hand,
let it fall down, whatever you were holding,
let it lie until the day after, let it go,
let it lie until it is blown to the river;

do not look back to see whose hand
finds it, or where it is hidden again when found.

INCIPIT HODIE

for Phoenix Alexander Woods, born 18.iv.2013

When you fell into our language
like a fish into water,
no wonder you were blinded by the splash you made.

We wiped our eyes
but for you it took longer,
it sprayed like feathers around you while you tried

making out the noises. And
slowly the stream ran calmer
though it took you a while to trust your ears and eyes.

How are you supposed
to grasp the water's flow?
But look, those flourishes are pebbles and fish.

Fish are slipping away,
the water is clear and still;
when you reach for words they will be hard like pebbles in your hand.

THE BINDING

When the train stops at the station he stands up,
moves to the corridor window, looks out and up
at a stone house quite close to the line.

With a stumbling ruin behind it, how it intrigues—
a view suggesting it belongs here,
and yet holds something strange. When I ask,

he says, Yes, I lived there once. I admire
the plain reticent outside. Yes. And do
people live there now? Oh yes, he says,

they have to stay, they have the bindery
and the herd. All that is still going on.
And as long as they stay there nothing will change.

You can see the big press for flattening the books in the shed.
Or at least I can, because I know it is there.

THREE SKELLIGS POEMS

IN THE STORM

What am I doing here, says the old strong voice,
the wave reaching and snatching
around the pinnacles, faltering and returning
to fling its quilt across the sloping stone
where in the softer days the seal took a rest;
so it wells up, squirting up roses in its fall,
trying again, the awful repeated recoil,
and where is truth under the slamming and roaring,
it wants to know, and *where,*
where is pity now? Gone below,
wiped from the view, and indeed
what has happened to time, as the day's news
is repeated, bellowing like the storm?

TRACKING THE PUFFINS IN FLIGHT FROM CANADA

No, not yet dawn. A shifting
intensity of dark. A deserted room. Inside,
screens take dictation from satellites. They twitch,

they go still. The storm beaten flock
signals again, a scattered fistful, drifting.

Labelled like seeds by species, their losses slide
into statistics.
                                        The gale of wind
they are crossing blows still fiercer
up the Beaufort scale.
                                        Then they fade away

. . . for now. Some day we will count their soft squeaks
in burrows, their whispers to the little fish, blind
under sand. Not yet,
                                        though here it is clear day.

OUTDOORS

In summer the rain falls slowly at the junction,
the bushes have grown, hiding the station sign,
the holly tree we knew so well is taller
so the clock on the town hall tower no longer tells us the time—

nobody thinks we'll go on our travels again:
hunger and cold and carrying loads are all
far away, the wind and the birds famished complaint,
far as the moving tanker on the grey horizon, as hardly gained;
until the morning when the mist rises at six,
the shadows lie flat, a thrush on a branch speaks his mind,
somewhere a boat swings away from the stone steps,
an engine kicks and stammers again until it fires.

SOMEWHERE CALLED GOOSE BAY

Just looking at the map in the long cold corridor
before the door opens for breakfast, I can see
how countries are nibbled out of continents,
their edges footholds to scramble ashore,
how they bite a coastline, give a name to a harbour—
something flew up reminding one of his home—
or an inland name—*Omaha beach!* Or
calling a whole stretch *le côte d'ivoire.*

Long tables in the refectory, a scrambled icon,
where a third hand surfacing on a Madonna breast
seizes a leg askew, its prehistoric sandal
intruding like a memory in the silver plating—but how
to cope at all with the past, since to my own mind
I appear to have been born in 1870
and schooled in 1689? I am stranded
in the pilgrim hostel where the only advice
I have been given is not to comment
on the goat's hair in the butter, if indeed
it is fair to call it butter. Presently

a spruce old woman—I have seen her photograph—
is to come and inform me about the last four
millennia. We will work at a clean corner
of the high table. I will drag her a chair.
For the moment there is nobody here except me
and the man who stands by the door. I've asked him
why it should be *goose,* he said what is a goose?
He says *Eat it up. You've surely paid for it.*

FROM UP HERE

The forest floats over the land,
the island slides across the sea;
they appear less firm than the shadow
cast by the plume of steam
voluminous over the power station:

nothing stable except for the gleam:
a flame distilled, neat
as the glare of the lighthouse, pointing,
speaking directly as the sun
to the eye it beckons, its brief

slanted tale of deep distance
surfacing for the instant: this
is real, it says, like
the hours of your past,
those roots with their population
of slugs and slaters.

INDOORS

Look in the iced-up glass:
can you read the shadowy blotches?
Are those fish, skeletal boats
learning low tide?

The alabaster lamp reflects
almost the whole dark day, measuring
light on the veined stone fireplace,
its curdled white and grey

the map of a language
spilling across a border
words retreating back in the throat,
the tight mountainous enclave,

as in the five days she lay without a word,
five glasses of milk huddled on a shelf,
congealed, the sun of a winter afternoon
breaking through curtains, piercing the shining whey.

FAINFALL

It's dawn, she opens the door to the yard.
Twilight is framed. A pillow of fog.
No sign of the cat. She stands there, inhaling fog;
this is the time when she is almost at ease.

Something stirs, a binding slipped
gently slides down. Is she alone
in her house? A rustling answer
clears away to silence, which lasts and lasts.

With the door wide open, still hesitating,
this is the moment when for once she feels at ease.

I USED TO THINK . . .

I used to think I needed to sleep—
it sucked me down
in long dreams of daybreak.
I used to say, do what you know
how to do. I do,
nervously I enter the ruined priory,
I greet the bats and pigeons,
I fall asleep,

                                and at once
roaming again backstage,
a new step feels higher than the old one,
the dressing-room door's rehung,
but the old tune played on the keypad
freezes in memory, locked
in the moment I wrote it there—

The knitted shawl dumped when the moths riddled it,
gone, the car scrapped long since,
discs and logbook, squashed in the wakeful mill
that once consumed the house keys years ago

saved from Cordoba: the tunes, though,
The Boys of Bluehill, Miss Canty's Reel,
the orchestral variations
with the lewd words added to the symphonies,
will follow me when I wake, if I ever wake again.

A MUSICIANS' GALLERY

It echoes with tapping, chatter, jabber,
noise converging on a teased out sound;
harmony remembers and at last
squeezes into a dominant, as the angel
tests the note he has found
in the depths of the lute, wringing
resonance from a tight string.

His body freezes alert, as a voice
echoes around the stars. The saint
beside him seems at once listening and singing.
He listens
                                        (and two rooms away
a man listens to his son
who is tensed around air, breathing
a stave that flutters and blows away—

to land at a wedding, where pipers clutch
bagpipes awkward as bulging animals
kicking to escape the clamped elbows.
The dancers hammer the floor: no rest this night:
the wedded pair sit steady. At another wedding,

the fluteplayer on a cramped balcony dangles a leg
over the rail, still playing.)
                                        Who is listening,

who can catch the lost bar? The f-shaped hole
on the cubist violin swallows it up until
the fiddler's return to haul it out, bend
her shoulders in a crouch, alert for the signal
to release the note again, matching
the wedding racket and the heavenly echo
calling to the angel to let his own note sound.

It is not natural for an angel,
but he must do it, the long note pushing him
into a body. Now the feet first learn
the push, the calf muscle stretching, the heel
groping for purchase to fit the vibrating ground.
This is where he finds presence, the tug and pressure,
flesh holding the music in place, company.

STABAT MATER

At last the page is peeled away,
the last page, like a covering from a wound,
and the transparent sheet beneath is another page
on which is written, '*You have no enemy*'.
—Just look. It is damage itself, and what lights up
the scarred flesh to the view
of the flinching eye, of the one
who saw it all and let us know, in words
we can't read rightly, until touch teaches—

as you can only find out by pushing
forward in the crowd
until your body is pressed
flat against the glass.
Behind the glass is the shadow of suffering,
and it shivers because it feels your touch,
it's alive. But others are pressing
behind, and you must move along,
and when you look back
to the house of mourning
the shutters inside shutters have closed
down, folded, each one with a day's date.

When the calendar was in its force
they all fitted together
as the leaves fit the tree
of atrocities, and even now
you can still hear the elation
of the strings, their long hopping
as the alto fills her lungs
to lead off *Stabat Mater*.

THE BURDEN OF CLOTH

The one playing the Cardinal is attended
by troops of acolytes to carry the loaded train.
The light pauses on the fine wristbands,
on the stem glass held high, the tight lip,
the sip and sniff that condemns. The director
calls time, everyone struggles out of the skirts

—and still it's not clear which one is the star player.
But they've gone, and the clothes are abandoned in piles:
the nuns' veiling, the calico painted with wild scenes,
the lace all full of holes. The studio curtains
are lined and patched at random to stifle sound,
but a window falls open somewhere and down they come tumbling.

There like the ranged cumuli they must wait looming
until someone comes to carry them all away.
—But who can it be, and is it because of the colours,
ghosts of burgundy, pale roses, that misted white,
that he stands there, shuddering like a flame wedded
to its candle, guarding a greyness at its core, waiting,

which is why it seems so difficult at last to handle and stack
the whole folded history balanced on two bone shoulders.

WHO WERE THOSE TRAVELLERS

Out there at the edge of the stubble field
slipping past, in pairs or singly, their gait
betrays them, the cloistered shuffle:

an old recognition, like fear
persisting as the lost path winding
in shade refuses, regains

its rutted dust each third summer.
Something has intervened, they are not
elemental as before, exile has changed them;

they are thin as air, as a leaf that has stayed
a century inside a book. They slip like knives
behind the arcades of thistle, on their way

to the emptied shrine. Only the soldiers
in their chopper can see where the grass changes colour
over the foundations. They take aim, and

the moving figures fade from the earth one by one.

HERE

A note on the table. Your aunt will be here
soon. He spends an hour in the wrong chair reading
her coloured magazines under a red rug.

His mother is coming here. Soon—when she finishes
talking to the nurses. The house is clean and bare,
a knife clangs on the stove, his aunt has decided

she'd better feed him. The long room upstairs
he will sleep in tonight is empty, a space
grief has hollowed. His own place, a home hollowed

to fit him, as a bird in its equal nest,
as a tortoise encased in its tortoiseshell,
expelled him into ordinary time

which is a long time, and travels a long way
to bring him to the edge, from where, looking back,
he can see the chair, and the red rug, the coloured

covers of the magazines, and everything that followed.

THE ORCHESTRA AGAIN

1

As in the story, a helmet floating
                                        half sunk in the mountain pool
where the rough stream falls
                                        and pushes the dead leaves
flapping at the brink,
                                        a mouthful of cold water
from a rusty cup.
                                        Could that have been his, she wondered.

The bell of brass on the stones.

2

An echo rouses the bright chords
when the wind section veers about and then
goes skittering downstairs, until
the strings respond, forging boldly uphill—

Is that you? I have lived another twenty-odd years
with the kettledrum knocking, the chuckle
of the woodblock like water over stones
that taste of brass in my mouth, waiting—

I have lived as all do now, in a fragile, woven
tower of sound that pauses sometimes
until the first violins enter together, they climb
the tower stairs and they climb again, then,

at last, silence. I wait for the voice
that tells me if it's your bow arm that I heard,
your scored fingers that played, lost
in the ensemble, playing to lose, or better

pianissimo, to be lost in the ensemble.

THE KNOT

When the house is dark and the air
quiet for a minute,
then past the window flits
that winging shape like a burning bird
that shoots back on its track and away
again, springing.

The evening fire
crackles now, the flame slips along the kindling,
the baby flames begin to grasp, they bravely reach,
while the air outside is as clear as water,
and the flying thing is here again, it comes back as if
to a knot that will not loosen, or the small
disturbance in the stream that reveals the snag,

back to that knot whispering in water that shuddered
past my knee, a clutching—
little waves like double quotes—

when the surface of the water glittered like a Christmas tree
and after twenty-one years the hanging glass butterfly
that I bought in the December market slithered away,
lost itself, loosed the knot and fell into its freedom.

DIRECTION

Searching about again to find my father
I must take a step backwards, for in the time
since last I saw him he has moved and changed
more than in all of his life—

he is a mountain becoming a mountain range,
a sliding dance of peaks, their names picked from his list:
the words remembered from the internment camp
that gave him his phobia of candles, his cardplaying codes,
the pipe he never smoked with its ivory bowl.

As he believed that foreign words were real,
their declension revealing even what crawled away
refusing to be learned—in that belief

so many troubles he shed, he leaves
me what I would leave behind for you:

they need not last forever;
they need not lay you forever low.

ANNE STREET

I still find the matches holding her place
in Gay's *Fables*, or Hobbes. The spines have suffered.
Those days, she worked at a desk on the landing, slept
on a sofa, her glass at hand. She cooked from expensive tins
in a stairwell kitchen. The strutting pigeons nested
against the chimney, where her chair caught the balcony sun.
John slept in the orderly bedroom. Who gave them
a gallon of twenty-year-old Jameson as a wedding present?
She met a man in the alley exposing his private parts
(which she told me were not at all undersized) and tried
persuading him to join her, and meet her friend the psychiatrist
in the corner lounge. That was kind. Now I would ask her
what had happened, that she was in such disarray, as one
might search for a defence. But she had done no wrong.

JULIETTE RYAN AND THE CEMENT MIXER

The world is beauty and order,
beauty that springs from order,
but more, it is a breathing surface a rippling
a fragrance like spice enticing from the kitchen—
a pulse beating behind the embroidered veil,
a branch spreading leaves against sky,
displayed like hair on a pillow,

a pulse like the one that lay beneath
a heaving, shining grey sludge of concrete in the mixer
as the blades revolved inside,
so that she reached out her hand
as if to touch.
                        But her brother grabbed
her elbow in case she did touch and finished
losing the hand.
                          I want like her to touch,

as if reaching out to lay my hand on velvet
or on the skin of a muscular chest
                                        or as Byron,

after travelling through four cantos, and eight years,
through four hundred and ninety-five Spenserian stanzas,
and across Europe and Turkey, so at last
he could finish with the pilgrim Harold and meet himself as a child,
said
that he laid his hand on the mane of the dark blue sea.

YOUTH

I might go back to the place
where I was young. This wide terminal city
—and I've lived so much longer here—
fills up with corners; I turn,
all I have done combines to excavate
a channelled maze where I am escaping home.

When I had to walk past their house
on the way to the hospital I looked
straight ahead, I spent the day
avoiding the windows, while
wheels unwound the corridors.
Going home past the philanthropic flats

I saw where the baked red frieze unwinds
the date in flourished numbers,
a cloak of soot sealing it—
it does not want to be looked at:
the floating curls melt away; the flowing hands
curve, do not grasp, not quite;
                                                  the paid line

almost lost quivers, there still,
as a child going off down a hill
turns at the curve of a crescent,
dissolving in light, in the view
from where her aunt sits marking her piebald
galleys on her porch: turns again, and shouts goodbye.

JUDGEMENT DAY

For once, here's a subject where no corner is left
for a cat or a lion, there's no shelf
for a parked cardinal's hat, no neat
stack of wood for winter, no tools
tidy on their hooks.
                                        Nobody calmly
pouring wine or hoisting a weighty barrel,
not even a window or a door to admit
light from a garden or a bare yard—
only rising bodies and falling, and odd blown scraps,
or bolts unrolling, of coloured cloths,
wide falls or skimped ends.

Is this where they were bound, the robed
processions of my childhood that wound past
open doors with hallstands, area gates,
narrow entries, wisely departing cats?
Away from every angle, every weight
sinking into our lives like the mark
of a body in a bed? To this great quarrel where
nothing is real, only the teeth and the bite
and the cascading remnants
that curtain away all that has passed?

THE SIGNORELLI MOMENT

She's back. Key in the door,
Dr Proteus feels giddy. Was this the house?
Didn't she remember
a frescoed wall with resurrected limbs?
There's a thump of a hoover, a radio plays,
a dead person greets her.

She's dead too, she thinks. A smooth nude
salutes a skeleton and gestures to introduce
while another levers
a strong thigh-bone out of white clinging clay.
Flesh has fallen away.
Politeness covers,

Dr Proteus considers. She looks around
for the service entrance, and finds
backyard, rubbish bins,
a fire-escape. She climbs, inhales,
but something grips her by the ankle,
means business.

FINDING PROTEUS

Queen Méabh standing on the top of Tulsk
could see her way as far as the plain of Louth
at the start of her great raid. Harder to get back home
as the traveller found, harder to look back,
still harder to answer them, those cries from far away,
from the rock in the salty gulf, where nobody
hears them, but they yowl as loud as Judas.

I searched for Dr Proteus, I found her but
O, don't ask me for it now, I'm killed
with the lot of you, says the voice climbing—
she's spotted a crotch in the rocks where she could maybe
see further again. If she'd give me a chance
I might be able to guess the beginning, and how
everything arranges around it, my history,
and the bits that don't belong. Up there,
Dr Proteus hanging holds the perspective glass—
but how through all her changes and her daft
excuses, how to tear it from her hand?

FOR EAMONN O'DOHERTY, 1939–2011

(After Ileana Mălăncioiu)

It must have been quite a blast if it sliced
the side off that house. The rooms
are all open, tilted, their T-squared angles
preserved, the bits and pieces all astray,
and a tall powdery cloud rises.

The shock has blown old bills and laundry
across the floor, piled like leaves;
the dog's toys have fetched up in the sink,
while the old suits in the upstairs lobby
creak, askew but still on their hooks.

Pictures swing and find a level
where conversations can continue,
still quite aware that in each room
is a piece of a vast shadow, and
even his shadow is hairy, has teeth and warmth.

In one frame a crimson sunset is obscured
by a branch with crimson apples; and now
an apple falls and rolls, fetches up at the root of the tree.
The shadow's vast hand reaches, there's the sound of a bite:
they still belong to him, they still have the taste of apples.

THE DISTANCE

For Maighréad Uí Mhurchú

Even with her beside him in the boat,
he never liked the water, he fingered a stone in his pocket;
but she looked back at the town of Youghal
where she grew up, she saw the pleated wake
and the long lines delighted her, their fading distance
where a line of waves hemmed an edging of sand,
a line of houses crouching, and between

the boat and the land swam a vacant pool of light—
and beyond that absence lay a world, that was sold
for huddling doubts and envies. She would see
across the pub lounge where the ladies ordered brandies
the discretion of light, the indigo tones
of their new suits for Easter, warm as a plum;
she would feel the gap she could not cross again.

*

When she drew a line on the floor with chalk
and I stood behind it, I could see
how firmly shapes were herded, how they clung:
the stones of the graveyard nudging the steeple,
the roof of a shop pressed down by the barracks wall,
and where the stone steps crossed the railway-line
a dark tunnelled space opening like memory.

Across that pause, remember her. The crime novels,
the cigarettes, the bottle of stout, her back kitchen
kept cold by the damp cliff behind it, so the milk
stayed fresh. *The old tree whispers its news*
to the trailing bramble, the roots of the whitethorn finger
the founding stones under the ring-fort, whose shape
can best be seen in the distance, dark against the sky.

WITNESS

Why doesn't she speak when they ask her
what has happened? Or she could point
to the film, to the arrested
frames showing a man
bent, carrying something
far too high and various,
too loosely stacked, his life;
and the next frame showing
how he crosses the darkened surface
of the river in flood, how
on the slimy footbridge he's caught
by the gusting wind, how parts
of the load begin to slide.
The sequence ends before
showing him as he stands
holding the last piece
in both hands, so we never
see the face, the camera
never close enough to explain.

The light when she remembered
after the storm had passed

was clear as a day in Galway
when the rain stops, when the sun
shines wide on bog and lakes;
it fills her now with light
until she can't hold any more,
until her tongue cannot move.

THE SENTENCE

Go home and sleep, sleep for ten years if you can.
Fight your way through the dreams, no doubt they will come
hoisting their scenery, the half-painted flats that suggest
scruffy hotels, the dull coarsely padded walls
of crowded bedchambers, cramped stairwells,
where you will spend hours in odd company,
where the dead are awkwardly present, and the estranged
are close but do not explain their savage letters,
while the child you forgot to fetch from school
goes alone on dark bus journeys along the boulevards;

If you wake at last on that other day, on the far side of the dream,
and find the trees have grown, the grass is ripe as hay,
and the old envelopes burned with the other rubbish,
if no crouching orphan waits by your door,
you are free, though not to forget, you can bless the summer,
though you will hardly know yet how many summer seasons
you passed in those inner chambers under the ground.

A CONVERSATION

My thoughts are all a case of knives

—GEORGE HERBERT

Although the library is like a case of blades
every one sharpened and the sharpest closest to hand,
and although the floorboards are piled high, the volumes
a stair, sometimes a cascade, a weir with fish-traps—

because there was only one player of this game
played on a scaffolding that sprang up, equipped
with snakes and ladders and slides, planted
with oubliettes and excursions that led to chambers
open as in dreams on velvet corridors
lined with colours as strong as ink—the thread
guiding us shone deviant as it plunged
under shadows and surfaced, then lapsed
as a looped line on paper (the frame
comes into focus again, we are back with the shelved
and stacked books to prompt us)—but
there was only one reader, and this time
he has not waited to explain
the rules of the game, which will not be played again.

SMALL

A word you were inclined to: 'a small plant',
'a small, old naked man';
never used in a negative sense:
the small difference intrigued you,
between a word in Catalan and its Castilian cousin;
the dense closeness, the narrow gap
distancing the genitive plural in Irish
from the nominative singular,
the narrow vastness between a broad and slender *r*:
fear, fir,
like a small woman reaching up
to stroke a tall man's muscled shoulder,
as in
'*To Maria Spiridonovna on her keeping*'
a small gift: eggs and cherries, in Moscow in 1921—

and in Moscow six weeks after you died, as the metro stations
filled up with soldiers on the day before the election,
I imagined messages maybe flying home
in the small languages, in Welsh, Galician, Platt-Deutsch.
I tapped one out: 'Saighdiúirí i ngach áit.
Ní rabhadar ann ar maidin.' It bounced back.

I could see the small languages clustering
like swallows on wires but then caught like the birds
beating their wings madly against the mad cage
of the imperial tongue. I watched a woman soldier
helping a small old grandmother on to the train
beneath Stalin's huge high arches at Mayakovskaya.

TEACHING DAILY IN THE TEMPLE

(For I desired mercy and not sacrifice
—HOSEA, 6.6)

The crowd in its bunches, men near me,
some women hunkered low on the ground,
a child at the breast, one girl standing tense
as an archer focusing—why should I recall them all
(and even a thin man distracted looking away)
and still I can't recover the moment just
when he took and opened the book and began
reading?
            or so I gathered

by the way their attention changed.
I heard, *If you knew what the words meant*
in the prophecy of Hosea. Then the noise
of readying the sacrifice began. I was there,
and so was the column of the Court of Women
solid between him and me. The offerings flowed
into the treasury beside the chair, where
he opened the book.

If you knew what this means.
They were angry then and picked up stones to throw,
and he hid away from them, so that day he escaped.
In my memory there is an interlocking,
a clutch of enclosures fitted together: the burnt
offerings, the altar of incense, the loaves
of proposition on the table for the priests,
gates and thresholds as pure

as water washes.
The wall of the inner court was tall and blank:
a clean place, nothing growing, the water
from the spring and the cisterns running off
with the blood of sacrifice. The coloured veil
ruffled in the breeze. And in among them,
between those barriers, the book now closed
and the phrase I missed
still there in the coded
labyrinth I must infiltrate again,
the language of the scroll construe, hunt down
between those hedges an escaping prey
before night falls on the phrase, on the lips
that move in the grave.

MOSAIC OF THE EMPEROR'S DREAM

Found is how they feel, herded in his dream of sheep
crowded around him, warm but not quite taking shape,
crushed between bed, book and lamp; and then the walls appear
the tall gates, and more sheep that push into the town.
The hidden voice that calls them is his own.

They keep coming, their breath steams in tight alleyways.
Raddled on their wool are their archangelic names,
a high grid of orders shining as bright as flame—
they are so many, but known each one by its name—
he is shepherd and ruler with an imperial frown.

They are so many, they move forward like the waves
breaking over the quilt and the pillowcase
as the sea rises and the gates crash and fall down;
says the voice: You called us as sheep, but as angels we came,
and one of us is the swordbearing angel that will break apart your town.

DIEPPE, 1956

Fresh, I remember, like bleached cloth, like lemons,
fresh as the ribbons and cherries
printing my white cotton dress:
whiteness of ivory in the auction-room—
an ivory gentleman, whose feathered hat, curled wig,
his boots and spurs, all shone smooth white,
wore a hinged coat. It opened to reveal
'a triptych adorned with scenes of battle'
                                                            because
before the slave trade reached its height, it was ivory
they carried in ships (like that one, with ivory sliced
for sails, with hawsers fine as linen threads)
plying the Atlantic coast, so the workshops thrilled,
working the white teeth into that fine mock lace
to frame a miniature group of Calvary.

THE INCIDENTAL HUMAN FIGURES

A bunch of rascals playing with dice,
in this print of Piranesi's, are at home
on the steps of an ancient temple. The fisherman
is at home on the river-bank and doesn't see
the man behind him walking with a dog. The shepherd,
his long staff the only vertical line
winding along in the foreground of the etching
of the ruined abbey, trails Biblical sheep—
whose tinkling bells you cannot hear. They all say
This is peace, those ruinous days are gone,
the humble, ignorant, even the idle
can live safely now; these do not care
about monks or goddesses, they are small,
and over their shoulders towers the ruinous past.

What about the sailor
whose fragile craft is tossed about in the oil-painting
under some famous cliffs? He has been summoned
to show the scale, to suggest the grand force,
proportion, disproportion. What grand consent
invades his heart as the sublime
soaks him, and swallows him down?

EVEN THEN

Even in those days it has to have been the same,
in the first cities of all,
lights showing, early houses, guards breaking their fast,
a pale woman serving them,
birds arguing with cats or beggars. Then the insomniac's
long-desired consolation:
the accents of people in from the country with goods
for market.
City workers
leave worrying lives behind for tasks that have names
and limits, or put on shoes
to clean after somebody's nightmare. She can sleep
till noon, while early risers
drink up the air of dawn, while time is shuffled;
in some room the musicians
are testing echoes; just then the card-game begins again;
and, elsewhere, the grandmother sits in shadow,
very slowly shelling peas.

DREAM SHINE

When I switch off the light
the darkness lasts only
an instant, they appear

like women in their doorways
hesitant, brandishing
their dim lamp. The shine

reflected from deep snow
edges the darkness
of a hanging gown,

singles out a surface,
a beam sliding upwards,
a gleam suspended;

a slice wriggles up
from a fountain in the courtyard,
slips into the room,

finds itself a shelf
bobs beside it—
who would not prefer

to sleep surrounded
by these gentle intruders,
wrapped in their whispers:

Go to sleep, dream about
the mouse that used to watch you,
looking out from his door

in the dashboard, sidelong,
as soon as the engine growled
and the car moved on its road?

THE GIFT

A hand rooted in a pocket—
of leather and old fur, it seemed—
jingled all the syllables till,
offering the gift, reaching out,
it slackened its hold:
                                        the girl's hand
stretched and grasped, kept the gift safely,
walking, all three days and three nights
along dry paths, past closed houses,
fields of thistles and empty barns.

It was enfolded, covered, tucked
neatly away in its Latin,
clasp and hasp severe and entire,
the beasts embracing, their jaws clenched,
the human-headed manticore
                and the jealous angels watching.

She kept them from tearing her, nights
repeating rhymes of ablatives,
prepositions.
                        She saw a gate

before her: there was work and food
and a place to sleep. She waited,
still, for the urgent moment when
she would open the clasp, the day
when the deadlines could all go hang
while for hours till dark she handled
pages, reading the words out loud.

THE SKIRT

The young girl standing
at the head of the long staircase
with her long full skirt
of black lace embroidery
holds her precious fiddle
her long slim bow in her right hand.

She has never, nobody alive
in this town has ever seen
a woman descending stairs
with such a fullness of cloth
managed, or knows how it's done.
Her grandfather sighs, puts aside his graveclothes,

the spectacles, crossword, pencil,
to show her how his mother,
his grandmother, dressed a stairway
—how one skilled hand rightly placed
on the flowing, trailing herd
jerked all smoothly into a parade.

She starts to make her way
down and the risers behind her
all flower in shiny blackness,
glitter in gaps of lace
following her down along;
and when she reaches the floor it opens.

She treads on down, the stairwell plunges away,
her feet still find the trail, she still holds the fiddle
upright, the white flash of the bow fading.

PASSING PALMERS GREEN STATION

The train flies through the station; and here is where
for years I would step down to the platform
and climb up the long stairway to the road.
On it goes, past that other station,
where my mother lost one shoe in the gap, coming back
from the hospital where she'd left her younger daughter
among the dying. My weight on the same ground,
the rails and the overhead wires the same,
the labours of the bones. The train dips
under the ground, and for the last stage
of this journey I am close to them, to the gap
that resembles the dark side of the moon in Ariosto,
where Astolfo flew on the hippogriff, and discovered
that everything lost on the earth can again be found.

THE PERCUSSION VERSION

Music is why we live inside
these foursquare rooms, why we gather
to listen to the scrabbling and the sound-test,
the way the splash cymbal explores the limits,
vibrating against the glass, and the bell-note
rings and rises like a cloud into the ceiling.

From outside the house how different: I paused
beside the door and all I could hear
was a chair scraping into silence
and presently a soft step climbing,

a sigh from the upper floor, at which
in the room below something knocked just once
and the well in the back yard answered
with a bass vibrating groan.

THE WORDS COLLIDE

The scribe objects. You can't put it like that,
I can't write that. But the client
is a tough small woman forty years old.
She insists. She needs her letter
to open out full of pleated revolving silk
and the soft lobes of her ears
where she flaunts those thin silver wires.

She wants to tell her dream to the only one
who will get the drift. How she saw their children lying
every one dressed out in their simple fears. They glowed,
the shape of their sentence outlined in sea green.
Among those beloved exiles
one sighed happy, as a curtain
lightened and the grammar changed, and the wall
showed pure white in the shape of a bird's wing.

But when she whispered it to the scribe he frowned
and she saw she had got it wrong, she had come
to a place where they all spoke the one language:
it rose up before her like a quay wall
draped in sable weeds. He said:

You can't put those words into your letter.
It will weigh too heavy, it will cost too much,
it will break the strap of the postman's bag,
it will crack his collarbone. The bridges
are all so bad now, with that weight to shift
he's bound to stumble. He'll never make it alive.

SONG OF THE WOMAN OF BEARE

Low tide. As with the sea.
Age darkening my skin.
Even as I struggle
Age grabs and likes its meal.

I am the nun of Beare.
The shirt I wore was fresh
Always. Today I'm worn,
An old shirt sees me out.

The main chance, the money
Draws your love not the man;
In our day flourishing
Our joy was the human.

Human goodness pleased us,
Delight on our journeys
Wearing out days with them
And no boasting after.

Look at them now: they crow,
They claim, they do not yield,
They part with little, then
Boast of how much they gave.

Carriages, prizewinning
Fast racehorses, the gifts
Of those high days: God bless
The giver's open hand.

And now my body craves
Homing to where it's known;
Let the Son of God choose
The time to claim me back.

These bony slender arms
Of mine—the ones I once
Owned, how they used to like
Embracing those great kings.

As they look now, my arms
Are slender and bony,
Hardly worth the trouble
Lifting to hug young boys.

Girls are glad to welcome
May as it draws near;
This season saddens me,
Pitiful, an old one.

I don't join in sweet chat;
No bride-feast is prepared;
Thinning and grey my hair
Suits the cheap veil on it.

I don't object: a white
Veil covering my head
Rather than colours I
Wore in my drinking days.

The old attract no envy—
But what about Feimen;
I wear out old clothing,
Feimen is clothed in flowers.

The Stone of Kings in Feimen,
Rónán's hall in Bregon:
Long the storms are beating
Weathered ancient faces.

The wave on the high sea
Roaring, raised by winter,
Forbids all visits now:
High and low keep away.

I know what they're doing,
Rowing over and back;
The reeds of Áth Alma,
They sleep in a cold place.

The sea I sailed on, those
Days, was youth—long ago.
Years took my looks from me,
Cooled my first young ardour.

The time is long today,
Even when the sun shines
I need my covering,
I am feeling my age.

Summer of youth I knew,
I wore out, then autumn,
Winter that ages all,
I feel it beginning.

I wore out my youth first,
And glad I did. How would
My dress be newer now
If I had played safer?

It was a fine green dress
My king spread on Drumain;
The worker knew his craft,
Coarse stuff turned to new wool.

And I am in sadness
—Each acorn must decay—
I feasted with candles
But the chapel is dark.

My days drinking spirits
And wine with kings are gone.
Now it's a soft drink, whey,
Water with the seniors.

I'll stick with the soft drinks,
God's will limiting me,
Living God let me pray,
Keep me far from anger.

My dress is marked by age,
My sense is gone astray,
My hair is grey, I'm like
An old tree's withered bark.

My right eye was taken
To buy eternal land
And now the left eye goes
To complete the payment.

The wave at high tide, then
The tide falling again—
What high tide fills for you
Is emptied by low tide.

The wave at high tide, then
Falling tide that follows:
I know them, I have seen
Full tide and low water.

The wave at high tide—how
Silent my store-house now:
Once I fed multitudes,
A hand fell on them all.

The Virgin's son—who knew
He would enter my house?
If I did no good deed,
No one had refusal.

Man among the creatures
Is most to be pitied,
Never foresees low tide
When the tide is fullest.

I have had my high tide,
I have held to my trust,
Jesus Mary's son has
Saved me from low-tide grief.

Well for islands at sea,
Their high tide follows low
Water; I do not hope
My tide will turn and flow.

Hardly a harbour now
Seems familiar to me;
All that the high tide saw
Low water drags away.

ACKNOWLEDGMENTS

Thanks are due to the editors of the following publications where some of these poems were first published: *Cyphers, The Irish Times, The Penny Dreadful*, the *Poetry Ireland* newsletter, *Poetry London, Poetry Salzburg, RTE Sunday Miscellany, Salamander, The Stony Thursday Book*, and *Windows Publications: Authors & Artists*.

"In the Storm," "Outdoors," "Indoors," and "Direction" were written for *Voices at the World's Edge: Irish Poets on Skellig Michael*, edited by Paddy Bushe (Dedalus Press, Dublin 2010).

"Tracking the Puffins in Flight from Canada" was first published in *20|12: Twenty Irish Poets Respond to Science in Twelve Lines*, edited by Iggy McGovern (Dedalus Press, Dublin 2012).

"Fainfall" was written for *The Lighter Craft*, a festschrift for Peter Denman (Maynooth University, 2013).

"A Musicians' Gallery" was first published in *Lines of Vision: Irish Writers on Art*, edited by Janet McLean (Thames & Hudson, London 2014).

"The Burden of Cloth" appeared in a booklet produced for a reading to celebrate the 40th anniversary of The Gallery Press.

"Judgement Day" was first published in *Shine On: Irish Writers for Shine*, edited by Pat Boran (Dedalus Press, Dublin 2011).

"The Signorelli Moment" was first published in *Berryman's Fate: A Centenary Celebration in Verse*, edited by Philip Coleman (Arlen House, Belfast 2014).

"The Gift" was first published in *What We Found There: Poets Respond to the*

Treasures of the National Museum of Ireland, edited by Theo Dorgan (Dedalus Press, Dublin 2013).

"The Skirt" was written for a festchrift for Maurice Harmon, *Honouring the Word* (Salmon Poetry, 2011).

"Song of the Woman of Beare" was first published in *The Finest Music: An Anthology of Early Irish Lyrics*, edited by Maurice Riordan (Faber & Faber, London 2014).